TABLE OF CONTENT

D1415315

Dedicated to the Wednesday Morning Men

With gratitude for your heart for the Lord and your
commitment to grow in Christ

So diverse only God could bring us together
So opinionated only God could keep us together
So fragile only God could hold us together

With deepest thanks to Lynna

WILDERNESS
WANDERINGS

DR. BILL LAWRENCE

THE ZIGZAG LIFE

"Now these things occurred as examples..."
(1 Corinthians 10:6, NIV)

It was Don Sunukjian—magnificent friend for over fifty years, best man in our wedding, and chairman of the Department of Christian Ministry and Leadership at Talbot School of Theology—who first voiced the idea that in God's economy a zigzag line is the shortest distance between two points. I loved the idea when I heard it, and once I felt a burden to write *Wilderness Wanderings*, my first thought was that a zigzag line, really a zigzag life, is the only way we grow into fruitfulness.

Why a Zigzag?

The idea of a zigzag life raises a difficult question. If God is able to create a world in which the rising and setting of the sun can be predicted with precision every day for all of time, if the phases of the moon can be established for every month across the ages, and if the tides of the oceans can be daily determined right down to the very second, why can't He create a straight-line life? Why must we live a zigzag life?

The answer seems simplistic, but it's the only biblical answer we have: because of sin. It may be the result of our own personal sin, someone else's sin, or simply the impersonal principle of sin in our universe. The reality is, we live a confused and uncertain life because of sin. Paul tells us sin creates havoc and chaos in creation, and all of life teaches us that the tension and pain we cause each other stems from our pride and selfishness, rising out of our independence from God—and that's what sin is.

Striving to Make Sense

One major way we sin is when we try to take over life and impose order on our zigzag world. We strive to make sense out of what is senseless, often to protect ourselves from pain and also to overcome the innate ambiguity of reality. By trying to take over life, we make the zigzag worse. The ultimate sin is wrestling control away from God rather than trusting Him in our uncertainty.

The most important lesson we can learn is that only God can control life. We must trust Him through the zigzags because that's how God prepares us for the challenges that bring us fulfillment. As He leads us through our wilderness wanderings, we must depend on Him. A zigzag line may not represent the "easy" path, but truly it is the shortest distance to fruitfulness. The biblical concept of "wilderness" is a major metaphor for life, and the zigzag experiences of the Israelites in their trek from Egypt to the Promised Land help us understand how God moves through our struggles to grow us into maturity. There are as many different kinds of wildernesses in life as there are struggles in our experience, and my aim in writing *Wilderness Wanderings* is to show you some of them so you can begin to see how God works in our zigzag lives to guide us into fruitfulness. Come with me in the pages that follow to learn how God turns our zigzag lives into His eternal purposes.

CHAPTER 1

THE SACRED WILDERNESS

"The Lord is in his holy temple; let all the earth be silent before him." (Habakkuk 2:20)

The wilderness is God's original temple, His personal dwelling place where He called His followers out to meet Him and be in His presence. It was in the wilderness that God called and commissioned Moses, and gave him the Ten Commandments. Here, God formed Israel and guided Moses to create the tabernacle. The wilderness also was where God prepared David to be king of His nation and the prototype of His Son. God met with His prophet Elijah and prepared His prophet John the Baptist in the wilderness. The Holy Spirit drove Jesus into the wilderness to be tested, tempted, and proven as Messiah. Scripture also tells us that Paul's theological thinking was fashioned and finalized in the wilderness.

The Wilderness: Good but Hard

The wilderness is still God's temple and the place of His personal presence. He takes all of His leaders through different kinds of wilderness in order to transform us into His instruments of life change and vision accomplishment. In light of all God has done in the wilderness, we must recognize that *going into the wilderness to meet God is good*, wherever it may be and whatever it may mean in our lives. Many believers think a wilderness experience is something to avoid or escape as quickly as possible. The fact is, the wilderness only becomes a bad experience when we refuse to learn from God and trust Him for what He wants us to do. If the wilderness is God's holy temple, the place where He meets with His people to prepare them for His kind of greatness—and it is—and if the wilderness is the place where He proves His people are prepared for His purpose, both to Himself and to them—and it is—then the wilderness can only be good! The wilderness is a *hard* place, stressful and often isolated, but it isn't a *bad* place. Entering into the presence of the holy God always is a good thing.

Sometimes other people or events we cannot control take us into the wilderness. Loved ones such as our children or our aging parents, team members who create tension in our ministry, or a boss who impacts our career might unknowingly bring us into the wilderness. We do not cause these situations, have no choice about them, and don't know how or when our struggle will end.

What the Wilderness Is

What is this wilderness we face? In essence, it is *a biblical metaphor for those arid, barren patches of life—whether spiritual, physical, or emotional—that God takes us to in order to test us, transform us, purify us, prove us, and prepare us for His greatness in our lives.* It is those hard moments in life through which we grow in God's hand according to His purpose. Sometimes His aim is solely to purify our character. Other times He wants to enhance a dimension of our competency. Still other times He acts to prove us, to show others that we are qualified for leadership. Always His intent for us is good, even when others intend evil, as in the case of Joseph. This is why our wilderness wanderings demand great trust in Him. Just remember that the zigzag line through the wilderness is the shortest distance to fruitfulness.

Why the Wilderness?

Why is it that in all the beauty of creation, with its snow-capped mountains and verdant valleys, its rolling seas and lush islands,

God chooses the wilderness to be His life-transforming temple? Why is it that He chooses to call His leaders into such a forbidding place? Why make this barren place His leaders' finishing school? Because it is a picture of reality, an insight into the heart of His leaders and their followers. The physical barrenness and futility of the wilderness pictures exactly the spiritual barrenness and futility of His leaders until they enter His sacred desert temple.

No matter what flashes of beauty we may have—and the wilderness has beautiful moments—ultimately we who lead are all as arid and fruitless as the Sinai desert apart from the purity and power that God's presence produces in us. Until God transforms our barrenness into His beauty by teaching us what matters most about us as leaders, we lead in the futility of our own personal wilderness. Indeed, what matters most is not what we do with our hands, but what God does with our hearts.

The wilderness of life is God's cardiac clinic, the place where He takes us to transform our hearts in order to release our hands from the futility of self to the fruitfulness of grace. Once He transforms our hearts, what we do with our hands becomes eternally impacting through life-changing actions that bear fruit. We enter the wilderness in the futility of our foolishness and emerge from it in the fruitfulness of God's wisdom and His powerful weakness. We do the same things we have always done; but now the 5,000 are fed, the spiritually dead are raised, the disinterested are motivated, the deaf can hear, and the blind can see—all because of God's grace through us.

Once Is Not Enough

Our wilderness experience doesn't end after one time there. In some ways we never quite leave the wilderness because God will not finish transforming our hearts until we are fully in His presence, and He gives us our ultimate new heart. So we continue in our wilderness struggles, sometimes with lesser intensity and sometimes with greater demand, often returning to old places in the midst of our wilderness struggles now made refreshing oases by God's good hand. At other times we find new barren and fruitless places in our lives—places the Father has never shown us before—even though they have been a part of us for as long as we have been alive. When this happens, we know we are entering God's cardiac clinic one more time for heart surgery without anesthesia. There is no way to sleep through God's vein repair or valve replacements, let alone His heart transplants; we only gain the full benefit of His heart surgery when we enter into the pain and hurt we have brought to ourselves and others through our futile efforts to advance our cause in the name of Jesus. God is corrective, not punitive, in bringing us into this pain. The only way to break through sin is for us to be fully aware of the death that the wages of sin brings, both in us and in those we lead and profess to love.

A Zigzag

We move through the wilderness in a zigzag line of struggle, confusion, and uncertainty. Why do we keep returning to the same fruitless place? Haven't we been here before? Why must we come back again? How can this zigzag line be the shortest distance between where we are and where we want to go? Doesn't God know He's wasting our time taking us back to the same dry holes again and again? If He can run a universe on time, why can't He run our lives more efficiently? Why won't He give us people who are as motivated as we are, who want to go where we want to go, who care as much as we do?

When we finally emerge from the wilderness and look back at our zigzag line, we realize that it was the most direct route God could take in our lives—in fact, the only route He could take us. As in the case of the Children of Israel, the problem is not with God but with us. If we had trusted Him more readily, He could have moved more quickly. Think of how quickly God could have taken Israel into the Promised Land if they would have trusted Him. They would have gotten there in two years, not forty years. Here's what we must realize: God gets us out of the wilderness as quickly as He can, but never before we are ready to move forward. That may be why some of us never find fruitfulness.

God has a pattern and a purpose in bringing us into this apparently useless wasteland, which is to transform our hearts so He can bear fruit through our hands. Once we learn this, we can return to the wilderness at God's impelling call with anticipation. The burning sands of God's holiness can only be faced bare-footed, but God is there to comfort and heal us and send us forth more whole than ever.

The wilderness is an inescapable life reality—a barren, uninhabitable place that reveals our futility. We are impelled to enter it in order to be tested, tempted, and proven to be God's fit leaders. Come, let's pursue God's zigzag path together. Join me in entering God's original temple and becoming a sold-out leader who has passed through God's Leader-Finishing School, the wilderness where He conducts His cardiac care clinic and turns our hearts of stone into hearts of flesh.

CHAPTER 2

THE INESCAPABLE WILDERNESS

"I the Lord search the heart..." (Jeremiah 17:10)

The wilderness: barren, empty, lifeless, colorless, solitary, unending hard sand, rock outcroppings, and rugged mountains. Hot in the day, cold at night. Far from the action, crowds, life, and what matters. Yet, in the Bible, the wilderness is the place where the action is. It is where the holy God shows up, leaders are called, a nation is formed, and a Savior prepared. It is the place of spiritual warfare, the greatest testing, and the most intense temptation—but also, it is the root of fruit, the source of success. Every leader will spend seasons of life wandering in the wilderness. It's inevitable and inescapable. There are no exceptions.

More than Hot Sand and Unbearable Heat

In the Bible the wilderness not only refers to a physical place, but also it signifies a grand metaphor for life, growth, and preparation for supernatural opportunity through painful moments. It is the place where God takes us to make us ready to be used by Him in ways we never thought possible. Never in our most ego-driven dreams could any of us imagine what God has in store for us in the wilderness. Look at what has happened in the wilderness:

- Moses met God in the wilderness.

- Elijah heard God in the wilderness.

- Daniel stood for God in his wilderness.

- The Holy Spirit drove Jesus into the wilderness.

- Paul learned from God in the wilderness.

Virtually all the people God ever used became effective only by living in the wilderness in some way, whether actual or metaphorical.

Wilderness Avoidance

Young leaders often ask, "Isn't there some way I can avoid the wilderness?" Of course, there are *some* ways. You can learn from the lives of those who have gone before you. Observe what they did and follow their model or avoid their mistakes. You can listen to their teaching, hear their regrets, do what they say, and turn from their failures. Certainly, you don't have to live an immoral lifestyle, commit adultery, lie or mislead, get a divorce, or be harsh to your children. Avoid immorality, dishonesty and deception, breaking your word, the pride of defensiveness, or pursuing your identity-driven personal ambition in the name of Jesus. This will definitely help you avoid the wilderness.

The problem with young leaders is not what they know, but what they *don't know* about God and themselves. They know facts, but they don't understand what those facts mean because they haven't yet been in the wilderness. They have the answers, but they don't yet know the questions. The wilderness raises the questions that begin to make sense of the facts we have learned. Time spent in the wilderness adds understanding to our knowledge and gives timbre to the landscape of our lives. It makes us leaders in life and not just managers of projects.

Leaders of all ages don't understand what it takes to become a leader. They think it takes skill, and it does. They know it takes experience, and they are right. They also know it takes character to lead, so they seek to gain character through skill and experience— and that's where they make their mistake. Skill and experience don't give a leader character. Only time in the wilderness transforms a leader from someone who gets something done to someone who changes lives while getting something done because his life has been changed. Invulnerability has been transformed into vulnerability, pride into humility, ambition into service, and confidence in self into confidence in Christ. Now the leader gets his or her vision accomplished—not by using people, but by equipping people to become themselves in Christ.

Desperate for the Wilderness

The problem with younger leaders, or even with older leaders who resist the lessons of the wilderness, is that they don't understand how desperately they need the wilderness. Further, they don't understand the depth of our spiritual blindness, the inner deception that prevents us from perceiving the assumptions and expectations that arise out of our desperately diseased hearts. Until we have spent time in the barren and rocky places of life and entered into what this means for us, we don't realize the wilderness is not outside of us but within us, in our very deceiving hearts. Nothing we ever face is as deceitful as our hearts (Jeremiah 17:9)—so deceitful, in fact, that Jeremiah cries out, "Who can understand it?" God answers, "I the Lord search the heart and examine the mind, to reward each man according to his conduct, according to what his deeds deserve (Jeremiah 17:10)."

Fascinating, isn't it, that when God wants to measure the works of our hands, He searches our hearts? We think what our hands produce is most important, but He thinks what our hearts produce is paramount. The reality of what is in our hearts can only be revealed in the wilderness. It is God's great preparatory school. When seminary ends, the wilderness begins. In fact, seminary and the wilderness are often synonymous—not because seminary is barren and bad, but because wisdom only comes in the wilderness. Courses, books, lectures, and papers teach us knowledge, but only time facing our hearts in the struggles of life gives us the wisdom we need to lead, and seminary is one place where God can impart that wisdom.

Every leader must be prepared to spend seasons of life wandering in the wilderness. It's inevitable and inescapable. There are no exceptions. You can avoid many mistakes made by leaders who have gone before you, but you cannot avoid your own mistakes. Why? Because you cannot avoid what is in the wilderness of your heart. Until you face that wilderness and cry out to God to help you overcome it, you will be condemned to live in its barren futility. Once you fully embrace life with God in the wilderness, you will find the fullness of His purpose for you. So I wish you wonderful wanderings in the barren wilderness of your heart, as God transforms your futility into His fruit. Such fruit is inescapable if only you will pay the price it takes to bear it.

CHAPTER 3

THE IMPERATIVE WILDERNESS

"At once the Spirit sent Him out into the wilderness..."
(Mark 1:12)

Jesus was real. Radically, totally, absolutely real.

This means He was fully real God and fully real man in the same person.

He emptied Himself of His divine prerogatives, however; not of His deity, but of His rights as deity. On the other hand, He filled Himself with human limitations and human needs, yet without sin.

Because He did this, He desperately needed the Father and depended on the Holy Spirit. Now some may react to the word "desperately," and I understand if they do. I don't mean desperate as in out of control; I mean desperate as in the deepest need possible. We must not be afraid to recognize Jesus as human, as one of us. That is what the incarnation and the early part of Hebrews is all about. Jesus fully and totally identified with us. He was not like the father who plays with his children and pretends they are bringing him down to the ground, laughing with great joy that they can bring this bigger-than-life figure down to their level, although both children and father know this is not the case. The incarnation was not a make-believe event for Jesus; it was one of the most real historical events ever. Thus, we know that His humanity was real: His infancy, His need for prayer, His testing and temptation, His suffering and death, and His resurrection were all real.

His testing and temptation not only were real, but they made the wilderness imperative for Jesus. And if the wilderness was imperative for Him, how can it not be even more so for us? The Holy Spirit impelled (Mark 1:12) Jesus to go into the wilderness so He could prove Himself to be the Messiah. Long after Moses built the tabernacle, Solomon built his temple, and Herod built an even greater temple, the wilderness remained God's original meeting place where His worshippers went to be with Him in solitude and isolation. God's presence made the wilderness holy; but where holiness is, evil is not far away because evil has a compulsive need to combat holiness and seek to replace it with its own destructive desires. As a result, Satan was close by when Jesus entered the wilderness.

The wilderness was an awful place, the place most impacted by the curse of sin on the physical world, a place full of nothing...just as sin that promises everything, ultimately is full of nothing. And yet Jesus came here, with wild animals prowling and roaring about, with the angels supporting and encouraging, and with the Holy Spirit enabling and sustaining Him while Satan was testing and tempting. Forty days in solitary isolation without food, forty demanding days that tested Him as Messiah and led to intense temptation. Testing and temptation always go together, and at the end of those forty days, Satan came to tempt Him with three of the greatest leader temptations any of us can experience and all of us feel every day.

The first temptation—to turn stones into bread—was the *temptation to self-reliance*, to take things into His own hands and meet His needs apart from the Father. It was a temptation to doubt the Father and to act on His own because the Father was not acting quickly enough. When He responded, "Man shall not live by bread alone," Jesus declared that some things are more important than bread, even after forty days of fasting, and trusting God is one of those things.

Shortcuts to the Long Way

Shortcuts are inevitably long ways on the zigzag line of our wilderness wanderings. Taking control of life and relying on ourselves to meet our needs virtually always results in a forty-year, rather than a forty-day, sojourn in the wilderness. For Jesus it was far more important that He trust the Father's good will and resist the Evil One. Often we fail to realize that when we take things into our own hands and rely on ourselves, we actually submit to the will of the Evil One and reap his tares rather than the Father's fruit. After all, a starved Messiah is of no use to the Father, even as a failed leader cannot glorify Him. It's all a matter of trusting Him and fasting a little while longer. By saying no to the self-reliance the Evil One suggested, Jesus trusted His Father and proved Himself worthy of being the Messiah. When we resist the temptation to take things into our own hands the Spirit purifies us of our self-reliant impatience and proves us to be worthy to lead in the name of Jesus.

Take a Leap Into Success

The second temptation—to leap off the highest point of the temple into the courtyard below—was the *temptation to do the spectacular* and gain the success Christ needed to prove He was Messiah. Few temptations are stronger than the one to take control and gain fame. Satan tempted Jesus to do the miraculous to make an impact, the very thing He was sent to do—but not for Himself nor in His own way, independent of the Father and the Spirit. Satan tempted Him to succeed by self, not by the Spirit. What leader among us hasn't faced that temptation and given into it at one time or another? Those who succumb discover that it leads to more time in the wilderness and brings an unnecessary zigzag into our lives. Spectacular success done in our power inevitably results in failure, and our failure lasts a lot longer than our success. It may mean death in the wilderness as it did for the generation that refused to trust God. Better to endure obscurity in God's will than burn like a styrofoam cup in fifteen seconds of self-induced fame.

Do God's Will Satan's Way

The third temptation—to rule all the kingdoms of the earth—is an irresistible *temptation to power* for many of us. One of the major reasons Jesus came to earth as part of His Father's ultimate plan was for Him to rule here. Some day He will rule over all the earth, but it will not be on Satan's terms or timing. Only one person was worthy of His worship, even as only one is worthy of our worship today. We know we are powerless, but we try to find power in ourselves anyway. We don't understand that when we turn to ourselves for power, we turn to the power of earth, not the power of eternity. While we may not be depending on Satan directly, we are depending on his system indirectly when we seek our kingdom, even when we do it in Jesus' name. That's what makes power seeking so insidious: apart from dependence on the Father, when we turn to self, we draw indirectly on the powers of this age. Thus, it was that Jesus gave Satan His ultimatum: worship God only.

Purified and Proven

It was imperative for Jesus to go into the wilderness to be tested, tempted, and proven qualified to be Messiah by overcoming three of the greatest leader temptations we face: self-reliance, self-achievement, and self-empowerment. We also must go into the wilderness to be tested, tempted, and purified, and by this to be proven worthy of being God's leaders in Christ.

If it was imperative for Jesus to go into the wilderness to demonstrate His credentials as God's Leader, can it be any less imperative for us?

CHAPTER 4

THE SHOELESS WILDERNESS

"...Take off your sandals, for the place where you are standing is holy ground." (Exodus 3:5)

He was a man without a country, with a lost past and a blank future, in a troubled marriage with a son for whom he had no hope. He was just living day-to-day, doing the same thing, running out the string, nothing to challenge him and no expectation of change. Not much of a life, huh? That made him exactly the kind of man God wanted to be one of the greatest leaders in history.

Who, HIM, a Leader?

It's absolutely amazing what kind of men and women God chooses to be His leaders. No one would ever think of them as leader material until God chooses them, calls them, and begins to work through them. We look for powerful men and women, perfect people, heroes who can solve our problems, saviors who can deliver us from our fears. But God revels in selecting the most unlikely men and women He can find, strugglers all, whom He turns into world-class leaders so everyone says, "Of course he's a leader!"—making it obvious that God is the greatest talent spotter ever.

It's no surprise that God showed up on that terribly hot wilderness day when Moses approached Mount Horeb (known also as Mount Sinai). He was surely thinking that his life was over. In fact, it had been over for forty years, since that fateful moment when his effort to deliver an Israelite from a punishing Egyptian had been discovered, and he fled for his life. All his hope faded into the past; all his future shimmered on the hot sands of a barren wilderness.

He quit. He quit on life and gave in to what was available to him: the hospitality of a desert chieftain priest, marriage to the priest's daughter, a flock of sheep to earn his keep, and a son whom he named Alien because that's the only heritage he had to give him. You can be certain Moses had no thoughts of delivering Israel; the only delivering he did involved the birth of a new lamb or the release of an old ram caught in a thicket. All he had was the same old same old.

Holy Fire!

Then something unusual caught his eye—a burning bush, common in that steaming desert where it was so hot, bushes spontaneously combusted and burned up in moments. This was different, however. The bush was burning, yet it was not consumed. "I must turn aside and see this," Moses said. Little did he know that he was looking at the rest of his life. God intended to ignite a passion that would burn in his soul but never consume him.

Suddenly God spoke. "Take off your shoes because the ground you stand on is holy ground." Moses realized he stood in God's temple, he had been walking in God's presence for forty years without knowing it and wasn't worthy of being there. So he did as he was told. He took off his shoes and became God's leader. Not that he wanted to. He thought his days of being a deliverer were over the moment he killed that Egyptian, his expectations buried in a shallow grave, never to be resurrected.

Shoeless Leadership

But in that moment, in that barren gray desert when he took off his shoes, his hopes were resurrected by the unwanted grace of God's call to shoeless leadership.

Whereas before Moses was confident he could deliver Israel, now he knew he couldn't. He stammered—and how can a leader inspire followers if he cannot speak clearly? He was a shepherd with the smell of sheep saturating him, and the Egyptians despised shepherds as the lowest of the low. How could he possibly confront Pharaoh if the king despised and disrespected him? He had been gone for forty years, and those Israelites who remembered him knew him only as an impulsive and failed leader. How could he make them listen to a failure? And he had no real idea of who this God speaking to him was. How could he trust someone he did not intimately know? Becoming a deliverer was too big for him, and he would not do it. He was polite, very polite, but no still meant no when he said it.

This is how God often works. He implants a passion in us, a vision for accomplishing something, and we're challenged by this passion. We are confident that if we can think of it, we can do it, certain we will be great as a result of it. So we act, but God leaves us hanging—or it feels that way. We fail—miserably. We dare not show up again. Nobody wants to follow a failure, so we're done. We are humbled, shamed, shattered, finished. With Moses, we quit.

Then God comes and says, "Take off your shoes." He is going to transform us into shoeless leaders. He's going to make us holy. He is going to send us to our Pharaohs, use our stammering tongues, and give us unwilling followers as He did Moses. He is going to call us to the unwanted grace of doing something we cannot do, of putting us in a place where we have to remain shoeless. It requires growing in holiness before Him, and becoming radically and desperately dependent on Him.

How amazing it is to receive God's unwanted grace; how overwhelming it is to live in this unwanted grace year after year and see Him come through when we never thought He could or would. He blesses us in ways we could never earn even though we are as unworthy as Moses. Like Moses, we too have been called through unwanted grace to do what we always wanted to do but never thought we could.

Once Off, Always Off

If you are leading through unwanted grace, remember this: never put your shoes back on. The day you do, you will lose your leadership even as Moses did when he was right on the edge of the Promised Land. What a shame to go through all you must to get to God's unwanted grace only to squander it by putting your shoes back on, by turning from God's holiness to your unholiness. Now that you're there, never lose God's unwanted grace. Be holy. Be holy.

CHAPTER 5

THE HIGH-STAKES WILDERNESS

As we grow older, we have far more at stake in our wilderness wanderings than we ever had when we were young. This comes as bad news to many because we think the wilderness is something we can get behind us. Who doesn't want a wide-open highway to a great life? The fact is, every great life includes high-stakes wilderness wanderings because, though the intensity of our wilderness times may come and go, they never really stop. Many of us have been given the impression that once we get past our first wilderness experience, it's over, and we leave it behind never to face it again, especially as we age. This is not true.

The first place we see this truth is in Abraham. He was well over a hundred years old when he faced the highest stakes of his life as God told him to sacrifice Isaac. Moses was older than Abraham when he faced his greatest test and failed at Kadesh Barnea. David was forced to run for his life and literally return to the wilderness when he was on the edge of old age because his son, Absalom, rebelled against him. Jeremiah, God's faithful prophet, was carried away captive to Egypt against his will by his countrymen when he was advanced in age. Daniel was more than eighty years old when he was thrown into the lions' den. Peter and Paul were both in their sixties when they were executed. John was past ninety when he was exiled to Patmos by the Roman authorities. The list goes on, but the principle is established: the older we get, the higher our wilderness stakes become.

Why is that true?

Three Reasons for the High Stakes

1. The realities of life

The wilderness is innate to life because of sin within us and all around us. Sin is a mental, emotional, relational, personal, and physical desert that scars every life. We were created to thrive, to be lush, green, fruitful, refreshing oases for each other, giving and receiving love in ways none of us now know. The thorns and thistles that curse the earth are a picture of the thorns and thistles that devastate our spirits. The older we get, the less we are able to deny the scars of sin. Our bodies wind down, and we have less resistance to the drives of sin within us. As a result, we are unable to hide our struggles from ourselves and others.

The wilderness within us forces us to face the truth about ourselves: we are not who we think we are—not even close. We discover we are insensitive in ways we never realized, although those around us have known this for a long time. For example, we learn that the short temper we blame on others is destructive in ways we never imagined. Our mates grow increasingly frustrated with our constant complaining and start to say things to us we don't want to hear, especially when they hit home. Our children make comments to us that we try to deny but can't if we are honest. We are denied the promotion we've been seeking for some time, and when we try to find out why we didn't get it, we hear hints of relational failings that anger us. "Why didn't they talk to me?" we complain, but in our hearts we know we would have been defensive, closed, and unwilling to listen. So we face the great wilderness evaluation of our lives. We have been productive and effective but we must realize that when life catches up with us and we are looking at the highest wilderness stakes we have ever seen, the way we respond determines the ultimate impact of our lives. This is when we learn that only grace can water the wilderness.

The wilderness can be beautiful when the rains come and the blossoms burst forth, but the rains come so rarely that its beauty is fleeting at best. If we will allow the waters of grace to flow in the wilderness of our lives, we will burst out in the fruit of the Spirit, and our lives will make the impact God intends for us. It may not be what we wanted it to be, but it will be far more beautiful than anything we could ever produce because we will become what and who God wants us to be.

2. Our purpose as leaders

We are greatly confused about our purpose as leaders. Many of us, Christian and otherwise, think of leadership as a set of increasingly significant achievements, a high-powered to-do list that, once accomplished, will make us matter so others will respect us. Certainly, leadership is about getting things done, and we do earn respect through our achievements, but it's about far more than that.

There's another major dimension to leadership, the most important dimension followers and God measure us by, but we don't always see it emphasized in the success manuals. We must understand that *one of the major reasons we are in leadership is to grow in public.* Most of the leadership literature doesn't mention this, so we're not prepared for this and do not recognize that the high-stakes wilderness seasons we face, very often in public, are a vital part of God's purpose for us as leaders. Very few followers know how to grow; they are impressed by what they see us do and think that if they do what we do, they will be successful. Still, they recognize some significant flaws in our lives but are willing to overlook them because of the good they receive from us.

God doesn't let things slide, however. He calls us to face these flaws in public. Through our evident struggles in the high-stakes wilderness, God transforms us and teaches our followers how to grow. At the end of the day, our followers will remember this about us more than anything else because they learned to grow through our struggles. They watch us fail, wrestle, and then trust God in new ways, becoming better leaders as a result. Growing in public is core to our purpose as leaders, and we can only do this as we navigate our high-stakes wilderness season.

3. God's aim for leaders

God has one singular aim for us as leaders, and it's not *success*, as most of us think. I agree that success is far better than failure, but the question we must consider is what success is and who defines it. Ultimately, God defines success as Christlikeness, and that is His aim for us. However, we must never mistake Christlikeness as passivity or uninvolvement in the affairs of life.

Christ-like people are not icons. They are not plastic replicas of the real thing, living in a monastery, never getting their hands dirty. Jesus was radically engaged in people's lives: He lived in the most restless part of the Roman Empire where violence was endemic. Daily, He saw Roman soldiers mistreat their conquered subjects. While He never mistreated others, He himself was a forceful man on many occasions. Christlikeness includes assertiveness, a willingness to make peace through confrontation while holding others accountable with a straight forwardness rather few have today. At the same time, He was the most submissive of men to His Father, and this is what God wants most from us as leaders: submissive assertiveness. Remember this, even Jesus could not become Messiah without entering into the ultimate high-stakes wilderness.

So it is that the older we get, the higher our wilderness stakes become. When we reach the remains of the day and all we have left to do is to sit and watch the sun set on our life, what will we see? A beautiful sunset on a shimmering sea? Magnificent snow-capped mountains highlighted by the lingering rays of the setting sun? Or a furious dark storm of frustration, disappointment, and anger? The answer to this question depends entirely on how we face our wilderness seasons. Will it be futility or fruitfulness? It's up to us.

CHAPTER 6

THE PROFITABLE WILDERNESS

"Man looks at the outward appearance, but the Lord looks at the heart." (I Samuel 16:7)

What would it be like to be left out of your own family? To be unvalued and know it because you are not invited to major family events. You are sent on menial errands to help other family members who then tell you to "shut up" and not make any problems. How painful can it get? Do you think you could grow to be a leader coming out of that kind of rejection? Of course you can, but what kind of a leader would you be?

Man's Look, God's Look

It depends on who's making a leader out of you. Many might look at how your family treats you and move on, but what if God decides to make you into a leader? After all, it was God who said, "Man looks on the outward appearance, but God looks at the heart." What if, despite your family's opinion of you and the way they disrespected you, you had the kind of heart God valued? Then your name would be David, and you would be on your way to becoming one of God's greatest leaders.

Those words—man looks on the outward appearance, but God looks at the heart—were said by God to Samuel the prophet the day He sent him to the house of Jesse in Bethlehem to anoint a new king for Israel. Saul, the king of chaos, was failing and falling apart. God wanted a new leader for His people, and He had His eye on one whose heart stirred His own heart. David was the left-out, undervalued, eighth son of Jesse,—the one who was keeping the sheep, while the other sons all gathered for a special feast with the leader of their country. They never even thought of inviting David to come to the festivities, let alone believed that he would be the next king of Israel. But their estimate of David did not concern God in the least; He didn't care what they saw in David because He knew what He saw in David. All his family saw was a kid. They looked on the outward appearance, not all that great for a teen- ager, but God saw His heart, really significant for a youth in his teens.

Even though David, the unvalued son, was valued by God and anointed to be the next king of Israel, it would be nearly two decades before he would ascend to the throne and become the ruler of the land. David had much to learn about himself and God. He had to grow in trusting God and earning the trust of others, as well as in following God and leading the strong leaders he needed to rule. The only way he could learn was in the wilderness, literally and actually in the wilderness: living in caves, being branded an outlaw, running from Saul, fighting battles, learning to lead, gathering the beginnings of a government and an army around him. As he patiently waited on God, he learned to trust in Him. This is the kind of wilderness you must pursue if you have a passion to lead, no matter what those around you may feel about you.

Anointed and On the Run

David spent well over a decade in and out of the wilderness from his late teens until his early thirties while King Saul pursued him. At one point, when Saul was struggling with severe mood changes and music calmed him, David was brought into Saul's court and became a soothing influence on him through his musical skills. After David triumphed over Goliath, he received praise for his courage—praise that elevated him above Saul—and the king became insanely jealous. He began to threaten David, causing the young hero to flee for his life.

At that point, David became an outlaw on the run, moving from town to town and living in caves in the wilderness. One time, when David was running for his life as Saul pursued him, he was hiding in the back of a cave Saul entered. David crept up and cut off a part of his robe. Once he was out of danger, David called out to Saul to show him that he could have killed the king. A man of honor, David submitted himself to God's anointed ruler and refused even to touch him, let alone harm him. Another time, David had to feign madness among the Philistines to avoid being killed by either Saul or them. He literally lived between a rock and a hard place in the Judean wilderness, even though God's prophet had anointed him king.

Everything about David's wilderness stay was unjust. He had done no wrong; he was the most loyal man Saul had in his kingdom who could have overthrown the king at any time during his unnecessary exile. He could have killed the king, and most people would not have held it against him. Yet David trusted God for His will and His timing across the long years of his sojourn and turned his time in the wasteland of God's will into the bounty of God's blessing. You see, God sometimes takes us into a wasteland to prepare us for His blessing. Whether it remains a wasteland or becomes a blessing is entirely up to us. Let's see the profit David made through the lost years of his life.

1. The time in the wilderness brought David closer to God.

David had a heart for God from his youth, but his wilderness season helped him know God better. He spent hours worshipping the Lord and focused on God's greatness in nature and on His faithfulness to protect and deliver him from his enemies. David was in almost constant danger for his life and could only count on his wits for so much. Most of the time he was beyond his depth, so he had to depend on God and learn of His faithfulness no matter what the odds were. David proved God to be true to him and grew into a man who lived by faith in the most uncertain situations.

2. The time in the wilderness revealed what was in David.

Others around Israel knew what was happening and saw David's loyalty despite Saul's unjust treatment of him. They knew he was faithful to trust God and watched him become an able leader. They saw the purity of his character as he grew in wisdom and skill, and that earned him the respect he needed to become a national leader.

3. The time in the wilderness taught David patience.

Because David was so committed to trust God, he acted only when God acted. He could have moved on his own, but he was determined not to do anything for himself that God did not direct him to do. As David waited patiently on the Lord, he learned one of the greatest virtues a leader can have: the patience to wait for the right time by trusting God.

4. The time in the wilderness enabled David to build his future leadership.

Many men, warriors all, were drawn to David in the wilderness. Perhaps they liked the free way of life he offered; perhaps they enjoyed the camaraderie of men and the military lifestyle that was theirs. Clearly, they were inspired by David, believed in him, and wanted to serve with him in leadership. Thus, David built his future leadership core from those who followed him in the wilderness.

5. The time in the wilderness formed David as a leader.

When he was forced to run for his life, David was a rising young star in Saul's court. He was surrounded by other leaders and subject to the restrictions that serving in another man's entourage would put on him. Once he entered his wilderness wandering—running from safe place to safe place, living by his wits and trusting God—the weight of responsibility rested on him. He had to lead or lose his life and his followers. Life in hard places caused David to shine as a mighty leader. Despite the daily battles, he learned to lead in the most difficult places possible. He would never have become the leader he was without his time in the desert school of leader formation.

6. The time in the wilderness gave David a national presence.

Once again, as in the case of Moses, the out-of-the-way place became the place of prominence and promotion. Perhaps it was because there were so few players on the desert stage, but the whole nation watched the way things played out between Saul and David and recognized the killer of giants as a giant among men. No one had more loyal support from his followers than David, undoubtedly because he demonstrated such loyal commitment to Saul because of his trust in God. It's amazing what people see in us when we think we are completely unseen.

If you're the left-out member of your family, tend to your heart. Do not resent your family position or become angry when they reject you. Instead, become a man or woman after God's own heart. Humble yourself to serve those who disrespect you and humble yourself before God to serve Him. Be a worshipper of God. Don't try to look good before men. Seek to know God and turn your seasons of rejection into times of profit by learning what God wants you to learn and demonstrate to others that they can trust you because you are trusting Him. Make your wilderness profitable, and God will give you His return on your investment.

CHAPTER 7

THE SELF-PITY WILDERNESS

"...What are you doing here, Elijah?" (I Kings 19:9)

Self-pity is the life-destroying quicksand of the wilderness that sucks us in, pulls us down, and squeezes the hope out of us. Often it catches us unaware and, because we are unprepared, robs us of all confidence and courage so we are left with loss of energy, distorted reality, and deep discouragement. Gradually we are pulled down, down, down until we disappear below the surface of life, all vision gone and our leadership lost in the sinkhole of self. What a pity.

Self-Pity Is Not for Wimps

It is amazing what kind of people get caught up in self-pity. We tend to think they are weak wimperers, complainers, failures who don't have the strength to overcome adversity and rise above their circumstances. In some instances, this is true, but not in every one. Consider Elijah the prophet who was anything but a weak wimperer unable to overcome adversity. His life as a prophet demonstrates that facing and overcoming adversity was what he was all about. Even his name, Elijah, meaning "Yahweh is my God," put him in a position of adversity. He lived in a place and time of Baal worship sanctioned by Ahab and Jezebel, king and queen of Israel, and he was called by God to confront this horrendous idolatry.

Baal, the god of fertility, regarded as the source of all life and prosperity, had been imported into Israel by Jezebel, princess of Phoenicia. She had married Ahab in a wedding designed to create a political alliance between Israel and Phoenicia. Baal worship involved the total rejection of Israel's true God and included human sacrifice, totally repulsive to all who honored Yahweh.

Elijah, a transplanted Galilean, became a settler in Gilead on the east side of the Jordan, a rugged and demanding desert. He became as rugged as the place where he lived, wearing a camel-hair garment with a leather belt around his waist. He must have been a shocking sight striding down the streets of sophisticated Samaria, the capital of Israel, directly up the palace steps and into the king's presence to confront Ahab. With no apparent introduction or preparation, Elijah announced that there would "be neither dew nor rain in the next few years except by my word."

With that he disappeared for three years—and there was neither dew nor rain as he said. Ahab became furious, searching for this wild man who had devastated his economy and threatened to turn his kingdom upside-down. When Elijah finally appeared, he issued a challenge to Ahab and the four hundred priests of Baal imported by Jezebel (who had killed all the prophets of God in an effort to stamp out Yahweh worship) to meet him on Mount Carmel for a contest between Baal and Yahweh. The challenge was accepted, the contest held, and Yahweh defeated Baal. At that point the drought broke and rain came. Ahab rushed in his chariot to tell Jezebel of the events of the day—but Elijah, in the power of the Lord, ran ahead of Ahab all the way to his palace.

This wild, rugged desert prophet, who had the courage to confront the king, call down fire from heaven, and who could run faster than horses in the Lord's power, surely would never get caught in the quicksand of self-pity.

Look what happens next.

Tomorrow You Die!

In her fury, Jezebel sent Elijah a message: This time tomorrow you will be like one of the priests of Baal—dead! Elijah was afraid and ran for his life. He who ran in the power of the Lord now ran with fear in his heart all the way to Beersheba in the Sinai wilderness. He went a day's journey from there and sat down in the shade of a desert bush and said to the Lord, "Take my life; I am no better than my ancestors." Eventually, after zigzagging across the wilderness, he arrived at Mount Horeb, the place where Moses met God several hundred years before. There, in a still small voice, the Lord asked him, "What are you doing here, Elijah?" In other words, "Why must I come here to find you, Elijah? The last time we were together was on Mount Carmel when I sent down fire from heaven in response to your prayers. What happened to the fearless prophet I sent to Ahab?" Elijah was, in fact, sinking in the quicksand of self-pity, speaking irrationally, telling the Lord to take his life—something Jezebel would gladly have done weeks before and saved him his grueling wilderness trek.

Elijah—the strong, fearless, powerful, confident, courageous, "Yahweh is my God" prophet—had become a pitiful, broken man shackled by a self-focused sorrow for himself. A totally self-centered man. Where did this come from? Did he have the illusion that he was superior to his ancestors? Certainly that illusion had been shattered. Did he live in the deception that his success as a prophet was due to him? That deception had morphed into depression. Any thought that his achievements came through his superiority simply demonstrated his inferiority.

A New Psychology Demands a New Theology

The same thing happens to all of us when we are deceived by our illusions of superiority. You see, Elijah had a nature just like ours.

He was a man just like us, prone to the illusions and deceptions of self, liable to fall when he thought he could stand. We, too, can fall into self-pity, no matter how strong we are. The stronger we are, the further we fall.

How do we gain freedom from self-pity? When our psychology is distorted and confused by self-focused grief, how do we find restoration? Notice how God responded to Elijah. When God wanted to change Elijah's psychology, He changed his theology. Elijah's theology was totally centered on himself. He was the only one left, and they were trying to kill him, as well. All the rest were dead or deserters. Everything was up to him, and it was too much for him.

God gave him a task and included some information Elijah knew nothing about. He had reserved seven thousand in Israel who had not bowed to Baal. "You may be the most visible, Elijah, but you are not the only one left," God told him. "Now get on with your life and get over this useless self-pity. You think much too highly of yourself."

We end up in self-pity when we think we are all alone and that everything is up to us. Little wonder, because God's call is overwhelming and we are inadequate. But we need to understand that God doesn't tell us everything He is doing; He wants us to trust Him, even when we think we're the only ones left standing. You see, *God doesn't tell us what He's doing until He does it!* If we need to know, He tells us...but only when we need to know. Otherwise, He wants us to trust Him and stay focused on Him, not on ourselves. When God wants to change our psychology, He changes our theology. What you and I need is a renewed theology that puts Him, not us, at the center of our lives. A theology that recognizes His sovereignty, faithfulness, grace, and power to do what we cannot do. We desperately need this truth and trust to deliver us from the quicksand of self-pity.

The Church of Self-Pity

The church also needs this truth at the center of its thinking. We are an Elijah church today, a church caught up in ecclesiastical quicksand and given to self-focused self-pity. The church's confidence is sapped by the cultural opposition of our time as we have lost our place in the sun of our culture. We have been invited out of the conversation in our society's public square. Our right of free speech is threatened, and our right of freedom of religion is under attack as never before. Theological shallowness is epidemic in the land, and our message has become a cloying, appeasing word of capitulation to the culture around us.

When many pastors want to deliver their followers from self-pity, they turn to psychology, not theology. We treat God as the Great Psychologist, as if He is Charlie Brown's friend, Lucy, solving problems for a nickel at a lemonade stand rather than as the sovereign Lord of the universe who is to be worshipped and trusted even when we have no idea what He's doing. We fail to recognize God's still small voice in those moments when we are tempted as individuals and as a church to fall into self-pity rather than to listen to what He is saying. It is not up to us, we don't have to take control, we don't have to solve the problem. Instead, we must trust the only One who can solve our problems.

We desperately need a fresh vision of the true God and His word of powerful grace that releases us from self-pity, both as individuals and as the church, and sends us on our way with our mantle restored. That deliverance is ours if we will exchange our distorted human-centered, human-dependent thinking for a renewed theology of God and His power to act in our world. Our deliverance lies not in political victory or in moral superiority, but in the broken humility that comes through the still small voice of God that asks, "Why are you here, Christian? Why are you here, twenty-first century church?" We are at the barren desert mountain because a watered-down theology means a permanent wilderness in our lives. We desperately need a renewed theology to have a renewed church.

CHAPTER 8

THE LIFETIME WILDERNESS

"But Daniel resolved not to defile himself..." (Daniel 1:8)

Rumors were flying. Reports were circulating. Terror was rising. Babylon was marching. The world was changing. Confusion reigned. Waves of hope crested and crashed with each new report. The hope was that Egypt, Judah's great ally and protector, would rescue the country. Then came bad news: Egypt was defeated by Babylon. Then came good news. Nabopolassar—Nebuchadnezzar's father, the king of Babylon—died, and the prince rushed back to the capital of his empire to be crowned king. Maybe with the press of his new responsibilities, he would forget about Jerusalem. But no, he returned, determined to make conquering Judah his first success as king.

What about the royal family and the nobility of Jerusalem, those who always paid the highest price when a foreign conqueror took control? Babylon's reputation was well-established. They knew that death and destruction rode with Nebuchadnezzar. Further, they realized that this terrible, evil king would come upon their city, their lives, and most concerning of all, their families. They knew that Nebuchadnezzar, the horrible idolatrous ruler, (his name meant Nabu—the god of Babylon—is my protector) would carry off their daughters for his harem and their sons to be his slaves. What terrible dread they must have felt as they awaited their inevitable fate.

Adolescents in Exile

The year was 605 BC, and the armies of Nebuchadnezzar marched into Jerusalem, the first of three waves that would eventually engulf the city. This first time they ransacked the temple and took the cream of the Jewish noble families into captivity. The next two times they would take more captives and then finally destroy the temple and devastate the city in their final conquest of Judah. All the fears of the noble families came true: Their sons and daughters were taken into captivity forever. What anguish must have filled their souls, what awful pain must have broken their hearts. Their precious children were gone, led out of Jerusalem into the abyss of idolatry and evil.

Among the exiles were four young men of the Jerusalem elite: Daniel, Hananiah, Mishael, and Azariah. On that awful day when they were forcefully separated from their families, these sixteen-year-old adolescents marched into their lifetime wilderness. They would never see their parents again, they would never enter Jerusalem again, they would never worship in the temple again. They would be forced to learn a new language, adapt to a new culture, conform to new values, create a new identity, make overwhelming decisions, face life-threatening demands—for the rest of their lives. They truly entered the lifetime wilderness.

Their hearts must have been heavy as they trudged across the Fertile Crescent from Jerusalem to Babylon and, with every step, moved further from the security they had always known to the uncertainty they could not know. While he knew what he was losing, Daniel could not know the opportunities he was gaining. He could not know that he would rise to become the number-two man in both the Babylonian and Medo-Persian empires, two of the greatest empires in history. He could not know that he would advise kings and tell them their fate, and, through that, gain their greatest confidence and favor. He could not know the opposition and danger he would face nor the amazing ways God would protect him. He could not know that he would grow closer to God than anyone could ever imagine. He could not know that he would see into the future of the world and describe empires to come and God's plan for the ages. He could not know that he would write a book that one day would be part of the very holy scrolls of God's Word he so valued and that he would become a peer with Moses.

The desecration of Solomon's temple and the devastation of his family catapulted Daniel into the lifetime wilderness, but the lifetime wilderness in the hand of God gave Daniel opportunities no man could ever dream of or hope to attain. His greatness grew out of his lifetime wilderness. Could the same be true of us?

Called to a Lifetime Wilderness

Some people are called to a lifetime wilderness:

- those who are born with debilitating physical limitations, who long to be normal, but never can be;

- those who live in places of persecution such as East Asia, the Middle East, and other parts of the world, longing for peace and security but seeing only the daily threat of arrest, torture, and even death;

- those who are minorities hated for their skin color, tribe, or language.

Many of these individuals are thrown into jail for years. Their lives are constantly threatened as they are physically beaten for their convictions, tortured in unmentionable ways for their faith in Jesus. Some in Eastern Europe, for instance, have spent half their lifetime in the wilderness of political injustice and personal bondage under Communism. As children, they have been required to do forced labor for the good of their society or made to stand in line to get food for their families, having to fight adults for their position. Their parents and grandparents before them knew the lifetime wilderness well and modeled the way for them to survive by God's grace.

Upon their arrival in Babylon, the three young men had to make one of the hardest decisions anyone must ever make. At a time in life when adolescents want to belong, to conform to the crowd around them, they had to choose between fitting in or ultimately losing their lives. They faced far more than social pressure. They faced the king's edict: eat his way, learn his culture, become his men. But they had another King, one whose ways conflicted directly with their conqueror's demands. What should they do?

Make Up Your Heart

Daniel went deep into his very being to make his decision, right into his very essence, into his heart, and determined that no matter what it cost him, even his very life, he would serve his greater King. For all of his power, wealth, and glory, Nebuchadnezzar was the lesser king to Daniel. No ruler compared with Yahweh, the King of his life.

As Daniel tells us, he resolved not to defile himself with the royal food and wine. He determined in his heart that he would obey King Yahweh alone, no matter what Nebuchadnezzar might do to him. As we make up our minds, so Daniel made up his heart. Daniel went down into his heart, as far down into himself as he could, to evaluate his options. He had to consider what his choices were, what his risk was, what the results of his decision might be.

His parents were far away in Jerusalem. He would never see them again, and they would never know the choice he made, but everything they taught him now gripped his heart. Daniel determined with an unshakable conviction that he would honor Yahweh and not Nebuchadnezzar. This decision, as irrational as it was in light of the dangers Daniel faced, was the one thing that led to his opportunities and lifted him to the heights of position and power, even though he faced envy and jealousy all his life. He never deviated from this decision made when he was sixteen years old, not even when he entered his eighties and was thrown into the lion's den. Daniel prospered in the lifetime wilderness because of an adolescent decision to trust God no matter what it meant for him.

A Lifetime Wilderness Means Lifetime Opportunities

So how do you endure a lifetime wilderness and grow to be a healthy human being?

By doing what Daniel did, by going deep into your self, deep into the core of your heart, and deciding that you will *never* under any circumstances accept your culture's estimate of you or live according to the identity your culture assigns to you. At your core there must be a conviction and commitment that is more important than life itself. Your culture will tell you that you should be angry, that you have a right to be bitter, that anyone in your situation has to be resentful. Don't eat the meat or drink the wine of your culture. Build your life on the foundation of a radical commitment to Jesus as Lord; trust Him for your thoughts, your emotions, your decisions, and your actions. Dare to be a Daniel. With this foundation in place, you can find the other resources you need to be healthy, productive, and effective. Without this commitment, you will never last in the lifetime wilderness, nor will you ever fulfill the opportunities that your lifetime struggles bring to you. Do not look at the hurt of your wilderness—look for the opportunities that lie all around you. Do not be paralyzed by the pain you feel or the memories that plague you. Instead, look for God's opportunities for you, and turn your lifetime wilderness into an oasis of great glory for God.

CHAPTER 9

THE GRACE WILDERNESS

"...I went into Arabia." (Galatians 1:17)

A Majority of One Among a Minority of the Many

Some people are a wilderness in themselves. Full of anger and hatred, they lash out at others like a fire-breathing dragon, setting the entire landscape aflame. Saul of Tarsus was one such man. Apparently a small man, based on his comments about himself, he made up for his size with a brilliant mind. Saul grew up in a devout Jewish family among the Gentiles in Tarsus, then part of Syria in the Roman Empire (now modern-day Turkey). It appears that his growing-up years taught him to stand up for his convictions and hold his own as a majority of one, turning all others into a minority of the many.

Educated in the greatest theological institution of his day, the school of Gamaliel in Jerusalem, he graduated at the head of his class, the brightest of the bright, highly dedicated and disciplined in his pursuit of truth. His achievements gave him great confidence in his knowledge, as well as in his heritage, and his zeal inflamed him for the truth of the Old Testament and the coming of the Messiah. Saul *knew* the truth, and he *knew* that no crucified carpenter could possibly be the Promised One who would be like Moses. The idea that Jesus of Nazareth could be the long-promised Messiah offended Saul right to the depths of his soul and turned him into a fire-breathing persecutor.

Not satisfied with the damage he did in Jerusalem when he instigated and participated in the stoning of Stephen, he set out for

Damascus as the authorized agent of death for all who professed the name of Jesus. His aim? To turn every assembly of believers into a burned-out wilderness of persecution and destruction.

The Christians knew this and awaited his arrival with fear and trembling. What could they do? Certainly those in Damascus heard he was coming and sought to avoid him at all costs. Maybe they could ride it out somehow. Maybe God would hear their prayers for protection in some miraculous way. Little did they know the miracle that awaited both Saul and them.

Saul, Saul, Why Are You Persecuting Me?

On the way to Damascus Jesus met Saul and called him to account for the persecution he was pursuing, and the fire of conviction burned out the fires of unbelief in Saul. When Saul became a believer, he was too hot to handle, either by the Jews or the Christians in Damascus. One of the first things he did was to alienate the Jews who expected him to lead them in killing the Christians. He was still the fire-breathing dragon Saul and not yet the loving Paul. He breathed his attack on the Jews of Damascus, setting them aflame with a passionate desire to destroy him. The Christians, not really sure of Saul, would also feel better with him out of Damascus for both his good and theirs. So, in the darkness of night, his followers stuffed him into a basket and lowered him over the city wall. Sometimes it pays to be small.

The Hot Sands of the Wilderness

But what could Saul do now? Forced to flee Damascus, he couldn't stay in Jerusalem, aflame as it was with the very spiritual fires of persecution he had ignited. So he did the only thing he could do: first go to Tarsus and then disappear in self-imposed exile on the burning sands of the Arabian wilderness for the next three years.

After his time in the wilderness, Paul passed through Jerusalem for a short visit before heading north to his hometown, where he remained for the next ten years.

Something happened to Saul in that wilderness season. Gradually, he was transformed into the man who later became Paul through an encounter with the grace of God. Saul entered the grace wilderness, and God's grace delivered him from self-righteous legalism to the surpassing greatness of knowing Christ.

Virtually every Christian leader has to traverse the grace wilderness in our passage from confidence in the flesh to confidence in Christ. The problem with many of us is that we can articulate confidence in Christ long before we can live it, so we think we know the reality of grace when all we have is the empty garments of right words. Until we've entered into the isolation of inadequacy, struggled to escape from it through our own strength, and experienced the depth of failure this brings us, we cannot grasp the fullness of God's grace.

The GRACE Wilderness

It's rightfully called the grace wilderness—not because grace is a wilderness, but because grace is the water that irrigates our deserts and brings forth the bounty of blessing that we long to experience in our lives. Grace means fruitfulness in the Holy Spirit, and only the barrenness of confidence in the flesh can prepare us for the bounty of the Spirit's blessing.

While under house arrest in the city of Rome, Paul wrote to the believers in Philippi, where he had been incarcerated many years earlier. He contrasted his past and his present, his old confidence and his new confidence. His old confidence rested in human achievements, such as his family heritage, his ancient roots in Israel, his affiliation with the theological elite, his passion to stand for God's truth by stamping out Christianity, his faultless self-righteousness—all of the things he counted on for a sense of identity. This is what made Saul, Saul. This is what ignited the flames of hatred and destruction in him and drove him to Damascus. Now he had a different drive and a new set of values; he had become a new man.

All of the virtues that gave Saul his identity were now of no value to him. They were refuse to be washed away as the waste of life. Grace had given him a whole new identity, a new way of defining value, a new passion that had truly turned him into a majority of one among a minority of many. Nothing else mattered except knowing Christ and continuing to grow in that knowledge, no matter what he faced. He could endure unjust arrest, unfair imprisonment, distressing jealousy, even gnawing hunger as long as he moved deeper into knowing Christ. He ran life's race with one aim in view: to obtain the price of God's high calling for him. This is the fruit of the wilderness of grace.

Forgotten by God?

It was Barnabas who brought Saul out of the grace wilderness and into the limelight. He played a role in transforming him into Paul. But it was God who remembered Saul in the wilderness, even as He remembered Moses and David and promoted them into fruitful leadership. At times we leaders feel forgotten by God, as if He lost our phone number, discarded our email address, and forgot to put us in the game—but He hasn't forgotten us. In the distance and silence of the grace wilderness, God is preparing us by radically changing what matters most to us. We no longer seek approval through our accomplishments, associations, or any other human measurement. We draw our identity exclusively from Christ, and focus solely on advancing His cause by pursuing His purpose for us.

The question we now face is simply, *Have we been to the grace wilderness?* This may be the most painful wilderness we ever enter because grace forces us to look into ourselves, to see ourselves as we never wanted to, to stare fully into the mirror of pride and competition, of personal ambition and self-advancement, to take off the blindfold of denial and see our sin as the holy God sees it. Sometimes in the grace wilderness, we will wonder where God is, if He's done with us and hasn't yet told us because He's leaving it up to us to figure it all out. I have been there and thought God was done with me, that He had fired me. Indeed, I would fire myself for failing as miserably as I had.

What I have discovered has stunned me. While the grace wilderness feels like the end of our opportunity to serve God, it's actually the beginning. He may implode all we have done, but He plans to replace our self-produced effort with a greater edifice built by His grace.

No wilderness is as difficult—or as fruitful—as the grace wilderness. If you don't believe me, just look at Saul, who became Paul. His change of name meant a change of identity, and that is what we are driven to obtain. Virtually all leaders are seeking an identity transplant, striving to become someone through our success. By grace we gain the identity Christ has for us, and we become the leaders He created us to be. If you are struggling with who you are, if you can't find God or figure out what He's doing, if your fruit has dried up and you wonder if God has turned His back on you, you may be in the grace wilderness. Take a chance that you are and tell God you give up. It's no longer you, only Him; no longer self-confidence, only grace-confidence. If there's rubble to be cleared away, let God clear it away. Then begin anew to bear the fruit that comes out of the grace wilderness. Let God's grace water your barren life.

CHAPTER 10

THE ISLAND WILDERNESS

"On the Lord's Day I was in the Spirit..." (Revelation 1:10)

He must have been too hot to handle, that ancient elder of Ephesus, or the Roman authorities probably would have taken him in much sooner than they did. Maybe they were concerned that, since he was so beloved, there would have been a strong reaction if they took him into custody. They did not want any unrest in Ephesus, the number two city in the Roman Empire. Whatever their reasoning, by the time they exiled him he was in his nineties, perhaps frail and declining in health. His wilderness was not a dusty desert but a small, rugged, rocky island called Patmos, just off the coast of modern-day Turkey.

The Romans used Patmos as a penal colony to warehouse their political prisoners. Domitian, the Roman emperor at the time, sentenced John to exile perhaps because he rejected emperor worship. Maybe the authorities thought the apostle would die on Patmos or at least change his ways after such difficult treatment, but he outlived the emperor and was released from the island following Domitian's death, a greater worshipper of Jesus than ever. The kingdom of Rome exiled John, but he was part of a different kingdom—one from which he could never be exiled and one far greater than Rome, though it didn't seem that way on the surface.

From Second to First

John was an uncommon man, worthy of respect from both his friends and enemies. As prominent as he was among the apostles, he is nearly always mentioned last in any reference with James, his brother, or with Peter, at times his ministry partner. He didn't move to the foreground until after the others had been martyred and he had reached old age. Maybe he was mentioned second because he was younger than James and Peter. Certainly, we know he was assertive in his youth. After all, Jesus called him and James the "Sons of Thunder" because of their temperaments and aggressive natures. They wanted to call down lightning from heaven on a village that rejected Jesus and thought little about asking Him if they could sit on His right and His left in His kingdom. Nothing shy about them.

As a young man, John was a small businessman, a partner in a fishing business on the Sea of Galilee with James and Peter. One day as John was mending their fishing nets with James, Jesus approached them and called them to follow Him. Immediately, they responded, leaving their father to look after the business. At that point, John became a man called to follow Jesus. Chosen to be an apostle, he was the most intimate disciple Jesus had. Along with James and Peter, John was with Jesus in every key situation, including His transfiguration and His struggle in Gethsemane. John was the one apostle who stood at the foot of the cross with Mary as she watched her son die in the agony of crucifixion.

From Lightning to Love

James and John were ambitious, aggressive, belligerent, and territorial young men. They were quick to stop a man who wasn't part of their band from casting out demons in Jesus' name. In those days they didn't know what Jesus came to do, nor did they realize that one day they would be part of the foundation of a worldwide movement. To them, if someone wasn't in their club, he had no right to use Jesus' name. Jesus corrected them.

After the first few chapters of Acts, John disappears from the pages of scripture only to reappear as the Apostle of Love through his

Gospel, his epistles, and the book of Revelation. As he aged, John became the most thoughtful of the original apostles, a man who moved from the narrow minded confines of Galilee into the broader streams of Greco-Roman thought without ever changing his commitment to the gospel of Jesus Christ. Thus, the Apostle of Love was also the Apostle of Truth who showed that Jesus is the only way to enter into a relationship with the true and eternal God.

Because John was both able to open his heart in love for all and focus his mind on truth for all, he wrote the most philosophical of the Gospels, while at the same time, in some respects, the most simple. His Gospel is built around seven signs designed to prove that Jesus is the Christ, the Son of God, and the way, the truth, and the life. He is the Light of life, the Bread of life, and the Water of life, which provide everyday pictures of what all need for life: light, food, and water. He took complexity and turned it into simplicity, all the while maintaining the dignity of eternal truth. Who would have thought that the Son of Thunder, the apostle who wanted to keep the name of Jesus for just a handful of men like he was, would one day write the most universal Gospel? He was a transformed man, and nothing shows this as clearly as his political exile on the island of Patmos. So what do we learn from John's island wilderness?

1. **John's island wilderness came as the natural climax of a life of growth.**

   John certainly remembered the day long before his time on Patmos when Jesus led His men up to the region of Caesarea Philippi in the far north of Israel. There, where a beautiful temple had been built to honor Caesar Augustus, Jesus asked His men who they thought He was, and Peter identified Him as the Christ, the Son of the Living God. Right there in the place where the Roman emperor was worshipped Jesus called for His men to go against emperor worship and recognize Him as the only one worthy of divine homage. That's what John did on Patmos: worship Jesus in the Spirit. As John grew in love, he grew in worship; and as John grew in worship, he grew in his willingness to pay any price no matter how old he was to honor Jesus as the Son of God. If we are growing in our love for Jesus and our worship of Him, we are growing in our willingness to risk everything for Him. That's the natural climax of growth in our lives.

2. John's island wilderness shows that advanced age means advanced testing.

We have seen this reality before in Moses, David, and Daniel... and we know that Abraham, Peter, and Paul faced this truth as well. John confronted his greatest test after he was past ninety—and he passed it fully and totally. All of his life focused on this eighteen-month season of testing, through which God drew out of John all He had put in him. What man has ever given more glory to Jesus through his writing? God put John on Patmos because He knew John would be His instrument to bring eternal truth into the temporal world. Wouldn't it be great if God could trust us the same way? Wouldn't it be great if God could bring us into our old age and use us to show others His purposes?

3. Advanced testing results in intense worship.

Perhaps the most important words in the book of Revelation are the words "I was in the Spirit on the Lord's day." John was in the place where God wanted him to be—in the Spirit. The apostle used the time on Patmos to focus on Jesus. Patmos was inescapable, but John escaped from the confines of the Roman penal colony to the limitless expanse of eternity through worship. He turned this time of intense testing into a time of even greater worship by giving himself fully to the Spirit. Testing has a way of bringing life into focus and of requiring us to make a choice: we can complain and get angry with God, or we can cast ourselves on God in new and deeper ways. While none of us will receive a revelation as John did, we can get insights into God and understand Him in ways we never could otherwise through the advanced testing that age brings.

4. Intense worship brings intimate understanding.

What gave John his capacity to look past Domitian and the power of Rome and see Jesus and the power of eternity? His utter radical commitment to Christ. Because of this, he could see past the visible presence of Rome to the invisible presence of God, past the powerful armies of Rome to the omnipotent hand of God, past the fading glory of Rome to the eternal glory of God. This vision enlightened his way, opened his eyes, and gave him hope when others had no hope.

Not every wilderness is a desert. There can also be an island wilderness that might come as your ultimate test, your most advanced test, at your most advanced age. Learn from John how God takes our greatest wilderness and makes it our greatest moment.

CHAPTER 11

THE SELF-IMPOSED WILDERNESS

"...Can you drink the cup I drink or be baptized with the baptism I am baptized with?" (Mark 10:38)

Striving to Meet Needs that Should Never be Met

Many of my wilderness experiences have been self-imposed. They grew out of drivenness within me—the fruit of selfish ambition, fear, and anger that created unmet needs in my heart. Those needs never should have been met. In other words, many of my wilderness experiences could have been avoided if only I had been aware that my drivenness and ambition—pursued sincerely, I believe, in the name of Jesus—were mixed with the slag of self-glory.

So it was that I entered into burnout and edged toward depression for a period of time early in my pastorate. I struggled with comparison, competition, and feelings of failure because I wasn't as good as others or hadn't reached the standard of success I set for myself. I did not understand that my fear actually was pride and my anger was anger. I carried inner anger without even knowing what it was.

Gradually, I came to realize that these feelings within me were harmful and that prayer alone could bring me release. By then I had been a pastor for probably four or five years, and knew I needed help from other leaders to be free. That's when I asked the elders of our church to meet with me early every Sunday morning to pray, and I gained deliverance along the way.

I realize now that my standard of success was self-imposed and not from God or anyone else. The bottom line is, it doesn't make any difference whether I'm as good as others let alone the best. I now realize that those wilderness experiences were self-imposed and unnecessary, and I am grateful to God for helping me emerge on the other side.

Fellow Strugglers

I don't like to project myself on other leaders; however, as I have talked about these struggles in cultures all over the world, I have found that many fellow leaders identify with me because they're in the same self-imposed wilderness. I'm just a little bit ahead of them. As I talk about these wilderness experiences, I find them responding, recognizing their own struggles, and seeking freedom. So what can leaders do when they discover they are in a self-imposed wilderness? By all means, find the joy of the wilderness, in the refreshing oases of grace. How?

1. Stop denying the truth about yourself, and fall on your face before God in prayer—acknowledging that virtually everything you blame on others comes from you.

2. Read the Bible in the light of your responsibility and God's grace. Make Christ your life—not only the One you talk about, but also the One you depend on to live.

3. Find someone you can talk with honestly and who will speak the truth about you. *Listen* to what they tell you, no matter how much it hurts.

While many, probably most, of my wilderness experiences have been self-imposed and unnecessary, they have been critical to my growth as a man, my sensitivity as a husband and a father, and my impact as a leader. I wish I could have avoided them, but I couldn't grow without them. So, I encourage you to keep on wandering in your wilderness. Sooner or later you'll get to an oasis of refreshing rest. But after you're there a while, you'll start over again with another season in the wilderness—and that will be the best place you can be if you want to become God's kind of leader.

CHAPTER 12

THE PARENTING WILDERNESS

"...do not exasperate your children..." (Ephesians 6:4)

Among all the books on parenting that are floating around these days, there is one missing. It's hard to believe we've overlooked anything, but we are lacking one vital title. I'm not sure how the publishers would respond to this, but in this era of self-publishing, they are not as dominant as they once were, which means this book might make it to the market. The title? *Parents Who Did Everything Right and Got It Wrong.* There, I told you it would be a best seller. Well, maybe not.

Unwanted Insight

Parents who did everything right and got it wrong most likely don't want to read about their mistakes. Of course, this sort of self-help book would have to offer some guidance in how to recover from their errors now that their children are adults and the parents realize what they did. Unfortunately, younger parents who are still trying to do everything right don't want to read about the reality that no parent can possibly do that, although sometimes we feel as if we can't do *anything* right with a two-year-old or a sixteen-year-old. Between a confused psychology and a distorted theology, we seem to be committed to evangelical perfectionism. Even if we never say it, we act like it and strive for it—a self-defeating drive if there ever was one. We must realize that no one ever gets everything right, especially parents. We try—very hard. We know what the stakes are for our children, as well as for ourselves. No pain in my life hurt as much as when I missed a goal while raising my sons. I wanted so much both to do the right things and to do things right.

Though the parenting wilderness can be hard, I must remind myself that being in the wilderness is not bad, even as it wasn't bad for Israel when God led them. God's purpose in taking us into the wilderness is not to hurt or discourage us; it is to purify and prepare us to for a greater future than any of us ever thought possible. If Israel had gone first into the Promised Land without the wilderness experience, they would have been destroyed. The wilderness only became discipline for Israel when they refused to trust God and take the risks He wanted them to take. His plan was to keep the Children of Israel in the wilderness long enough for them to learn how to enter into a deeper, intimate relationship with Him. Once they learned to do that, He wanted to lead them through the battles with the Canaanites into the peace and tranquility of a free nation in fellowship with Him.

When we end up in the parenting wilderness, God's desire is not for us to stay there, but to learn to be more effective than ever in raising our children. Once we have grown to trust Him more fully, He is ready for us to move forward in the joy of parenting. If you feel you are failing with your children, get some help, learn what you can do to change the situation, and take the steps you need to make the necessary adjustment. It's most often not as easy as it sounds, of course, and especially because you have so much at stake in your child. It may take more time than you want it to, and you may need more help than you realized at first; but God's purpose is not to make our parenting a wilderness but a great joy.

Let's take a look at some self-imposed parenting wildernesses we need to be aware of that can lead to significant strife in families.

Striving for Perfection

Nobody is perfect, and nobody ever will be. No parent ever raised a perfect child (except in our own eyes), and no parent ever will.

Striving to raise perfect children is guaranteed to produce pain for you and even more pain for your child. Often the effort to raise perfect children reveals far more about the parents than it does the children because it's all about the parents and their need to look good before others. For whatever reason, they must be right and can't face anything less than perfection in themselves, and they treat their children as extensions of themselves. This drives their children either to try to look as good as their parents or to go as far in the opposite direction as they can. Children cannot stand up under the weight of their parents' perfection, so sooner or later the pressures of life will break down the façade of perfection to reveal deep flaws that have been covered for many years. That results in terrible pain for both parents and children. The drive for perfection is one of the most horrible wildernesses we can ever endure.

Parenting is not about the parents; it's about the children. If it were about the parents, the Father in the Parable of the Prodigal Son never would have let his son insult him or given him his inheritance to waste. Apparently, that's the only way he could have the kind of son he wanted, one who was humbled by repentance and ready to live responsibly in the father's love.

Becoming a parent is the biggest risk you will ever take in life, and it continues to be risky as long as you live because you never know what your children are going to do. Children, particularly adolescent and young adult children, make decisions on their own, decisions that can have lasting results. Children choose to sin despite what we teach them, and they may even blame us for their sin. Parents cannot control those choices and raise a healthy adult any more than the father of the prodigal son could prevent him from choosing to do what he did.

The father certainly knew what his son was going to do, but he chose to pay the price of pain, a father's pain, so he could have a son and not a robot. Perfect children grow up as robots at best, automatons imitating their parents and never growing into their own identities. Some parents seem to need little imitations and not flesh-and-blood children who become real in life by learning to navigate their own wildernesses. Unless our children see us struggling with our wildernesses, they will never learn to enter into life and become real.

Raising our Children to Avoid the Hurt
We Experienced Growing Up

One of the biggest and most human parenting mistakes we make is trying to prevent what happened to us when we were growing up from happening to our children. Now, if we were sexually abused or grew up in an addicted home, we definitely must prevent that from happening. If we were sexually promiscuous or chemically addicted, we don't want that for our children, of course. But it doesn't follow that because we did destructive things to ourselves, our children will do the same. Trying to prevent what happened to us is like a general who fights today's battles according to the last war: they lose both the battles and the war. Our children are not growing up in the home we grew up in. Our home is different, our marriage is different, our values may be different, certainly our culture is different. Our children are not growing up in our childhood home or in our childhood world. We are in unchartered territory, but then parenting has always been unchartered territory. We cannot parent simply to avoid the pain we had; we have to parent to achieve God's call on us as mothers and fathers and God's will for our children.

The question is not, How can I help my children avoid my pain? Rather, it is, How can I help my children find their fulfillment in God's plan? They're not living my life; they're living their own lives. My mother grew up in a broken family with an abusive mother and a lazy father, and my father's dad died when my father was fourteen.

My mother wanted to prevent what happened to her from happening to me while my father wanted to meet a need I didn't have—he tried to give to me what he longed for after he lost his dad. To do this, they exercised great control over me and used me to meet their needs. I wasn't in a broken and abusive family and had a father during my teenage years, so I didn't need what they tried to give me. Eventually, I rejected their efforts and broke their control, which created great hurt for them and much struggle for me.

If you feel you must parent to prevent your pain from happening to your children, do so—but remember, they're not growing up in the family you grew up in. They're growing up in *your* family. Be certain you're not making your parents' mistakes, but don't become so focused on preventing your hurt in your children that you miss other needs and create unnecessary hurt in them. Parenting is a pendulum between generations as we bounce from one effort to another. We do our best, but all parents have blind spots that impact our children. When those blind spots show up, we must be humble, not defensive, willing to acknowledge what we did wrong and do the best we can to overcome it. None of us ever escapes from some part of the parenting wilderness.

What can you do when you find yourself in the parenting wilderness? Although this is not an exhaustive list, these disciplines will help you through the hard times of the parenting wilderness.

1. Pray.

When our sons turned thirteen, I realized I could not direct them the same way I did when they were younger. I had to give them space to make mistakes and learn, or they would never become the men I wanted them to be. I made a prayer list and spent significant time daily seeking God's wisdom and grace for all three of them, especially when I saw an issue that concerned me greatly. I saw significant answers to prayer that either helped us avoid the parenting wilderness or got us out of it before it became overwhelming.

2. **Understand that parenting is spiritual warfare and our enemy is incomprehensibly evil and ruthless.**

Satan does not see our children as the cute, innocent, wonderful beings we rightfully see them to be. He sees them as victims, ways to get at us and bring hurt and pain into our lives, because he entices them toward destructive actions—even addictions—that devastate them and shatter us. Pray against the Evil One, dress your family in the armor of God, hate him for all he is, and cry out to God for your family. I learned to pray this way for my children from Job, and I understand much better today why he prayed as he did. Parenting has brought us the greatest joy of our lives, but we have also known the wilderness as well.

3. **Know your children are a stewardship from God, not a reputation maker for you.**

As your children mature, look to understand how God has made them, what He made them to be, and realize that you do not decide who they are and how they will express their identity. You help them discover their identity and their future, but parents who try to determine their children's future may well force them to go in a harmful direction that creates resistance and resentment as they are growing up or great pain later in their lives.

4. **Love them for all they're worth and then some.**

Tell your children you love them every day—in fact, several times a day—and hug them every chance you get, even when they don't want you to. Grab your nearly six-foot junior-higher, plant a big kiss on him, hug him, and proclaim your love to him no matter how hard he fights you. He may resist it, but down inside he needs to know it. Whenever there's tension, never let it end without making sure your children know you love them.

5. Pray together with them and immerse them in God's Word early and often.

Nothing unifies and binds like prayer and God's Word. One of our neighbors told my mother when I was a child that if she taught me to memorize Scripture, I would hate the Bible when I grew up. She said my mother was overdoing it. My mother had a very simple but deep faith, which she passed on to me, and today I love the Word and prayer. Our neighbor was wrong. Just don't preach at your children when they disobey or you feel threatened by what they're doing. There are no guarantees in parenting, but we can plant and water the seeds of truth with prayer for years to come.

6. Be humble before your children.

If you're wrong, you're wrong, and when they're right and know it, you must acknowledge it. The parents who won't do that don't lose face—they lose their child. Don't hesitate to apologize and ask for forgiveness. Your children's respect for you will grow, as will their willingness to listen to you and obey you.

7. Listen to your children.

They may well have a viable solution to a family problem. You should not put decisions on them that you are responsible to make, but listening to their voice gives them a sense of value and respect they will treasure for as long as they live. It also helps them learn how adults make decisions. Becoming part of family concerns and participating in the resolution of such issues lifts your children to a new level of ownership and growth they would never have otherwise.

Nothing will bring you more joy than parenting, but all of us end up in the parenting wilderness at times. Remember, the wilderness is not a bad place—it's not negative to be there. The wilderness is always a stop on the way to the Promised Land, the way to God's opportunity and blessing that you would miss if you didn't spend time with Him being prepared for His future for you. Don't be afraid to go there as a parent, but once you're there, listen and learn as quickly as you can so you can move forward on your journey toward the parenting blessings God has for you.

CHAPTER 13

THE LUCKY WILDERNESS

"They will be like a tree planted by the water that sends out its roots by the stream..." (Jeremiah 17:9)

John Paine calls himself "the luckiest man in the world," and most agreed with him some years ago. When John was in the seventh grade, he decided he would be physically strong. He worked diligently until he became a superior athlete who played college football. Then he decided to transfer to a top ten engineering school and reached his goal of becoming academically strong by graduating *summa cum laude*. Upon graduation, John married his high school sweetheart and started his family. At the same time, he decided he would become financially strong and determined to carve out his way by starting his own company, the first of many that he created and built into successful ventures. All along the way, he was spiritually strong—fully committed to Christ, leading his family to know the Lord, running his companies in a Christian way, becoming a teacher of God's truth, and influencing his fellow business leaders with the gospel. John was definitely a strong man and what he calls a "lucky man."

All went well until about fifteen years ago when John noticed some uncontrollable muscle spasms in his body and a growing physical weakness, even though he was working out and jogging regularly. His symptoms reached the point that he could no longer ignore them, so he went to be checked out medically. After a number of tests, he finally learned the cause of his spasms and growing weakness. He had Lou Gehrig's disease (medically known as ALS), a debilitating illness named for one of the greatest athletes in American sports history who died of this progressive and destructive illness. John could see his future when he went to his new doctors: the progressive weakening of his muscles indicated by involutionary spasms called fasciculations and the gradual loss of all physical strength signaled by his increasing inability to walk or use his arms and hands, thus putting him in a wheelchair and eventually denying his ability even to breathe as his diaphragm became compromised. However, his brilliant business mind would never be touched. He would be fully aware of all that was happening to him as he lost a little more strength each day until the strong man became totally depleted and dependent. The lucky man had become an unlucky man.

When Good Luck Goes Bad

All the dire medical predictions John received eventually came true. He hasn't been able to walk for several years. He cannot use his arms or hands, his breathing is now assisted by a ventilator, and his strength is gone. He is totally dependent on others to do everything. The once uncommonly strong man is now uncommonly weak. Yet, one day when I was meeting with John and he told me about how he committed to build physical, intellectual, and financial strength to go with his spiritual strength, he finished by saying, "And today I am stronger than ever!" I was amazed when he said that. With all his physical strength gone, how could he be stronger than ever? The answer to that question is self-evident. The only way John has survived his ordeal and maintained his perspective and courage is by entering God's presence and trusting Him deeply. Despite his physical condition, John finds superlative personal strength through the Lord to continue to serve Him even though he is paralyzed from the neck down. The Lord's power has made him stronger than ever.

How Do You Do It?

That strength is well known in Dallas among the many who knew Him both before and after his diagnosis. Over the past nearly fifteen years, large numbers of his business peers, professionals, and ministry leaders have come to John for help with their lives. They marvel at how he has maintained his spirit and exalted the Lord despite his limitations and how he has grown stronger as he has grown weaker. They come to him to learn and draw from God's imparted wisdom. Unbelievers have made appointments with John to ask him how he does what he does, how he maintains a positive spirit and not grown bitter at God for what has happened to him. They ask him, "How do you do it? How can you give so much to others and be filled with joy in spite of what is happening to you?"

For all who ask, he has one answer: "I do it in the Lord's power. At the end of my will and my power, God shows up in a mighty way." Then he tells them how they can have that same power for their weakness, both for eternity and for time. Through his conversations with his peers, John has discovered that many have a distorted view of God. They don't understand His grace and feel that they must meet His standards on their own. Many see God as judgmental, not loving and gracious. Often they are confused about the way their wives and children respond to them and don't know how to resolve the conflicts that confront them. Many don't know where to turn with their businesses as they struggle with the uncertainties of the marketplace. Because of John's dedication to the Lord and his commitment to succeed in business, he has been able to help them greatly.

When Bad Luck Is Good

John calls himself the luckiest man in the world because, as it turns out, he doesn't think he's unlucky at all. That is why this chapter is called "The Lucky Wilderness." A company devoted to highlighting uncommonly inspirational people called Fotolanthropy, has made a film about John, titled "The Luckiest Man." John has certainly been in a wilderness, but he doesn't think of this wilderness as a bad place. Instead, he sees it as a transformative place where his heart was made whole. He is aware of what he has lost. He longs to pick up and sip a cup of coffee on his own or take up his favorite pen and write in his journal as he once did, or hold his wife's hand just one more time. He cannot do these things ever again. Yet he calls himself "the luckiest man," and he's not just saying platitudes. He's serious. He means it.

At the end of the film, John makes a statement concerning his view of his life and explains why he calls himself "the luckiest man in the world." Read John's own words about how he views his "luck" in life.

"There it was, not more than six feet in front of me, my greatest fear! I was attending my first ALS clinic to learn about all of the resources available for patients. I was surrounded by others, all at varying stages of progression of the disease. It was terrifying seeing their shuffling gaits, rolling wheelchairs and complete dependence on others; this would invariably be my future. . . . My instinctive reaction was to plea 'Please, Please Dear Lord do not let that be me. Do not let me live just existing like that. . . .' That was then, this is now. . . . This is what God said through His prophet Jeremiah from his book in 17:7-8, "Blessed is the man who trusts in the Lord and whose trust is the Lord. For he will be like a tree planted by the water, that extends its roots by a stream and will not fear when the heat comes; but its leaves will be green, and it will not be anxious in a year of drought nor cease to yield fruit"(NASB). Even in the midst of extreme heat and drought He produces abundance. Green leaves and fruit in our lives represent joy in the midst of adversity, peace in the midst of turmoil, and contentment even while living with an incurable disease. You see, walking with God produces not just living but abundant living! It is without Him that we just exist … God did answer my prayer in the ALS clinic that day—it just

was in a better way than I could have expected. While all of those things I once feared have come true, my life is far from mere existence. The presence of God that produces abundant living is greater and trumps anything ALS can dish out or negative circumstances could ever produce. Those of you who are planted by the water and whose roots grow deep by His stream understand why I now live abundantly, without fear and proclaim to be The Luckiest Man in the World! I count it pure joy in living connected with my God so that I may fulfill my life's purpose of helping others know and walk closer with Him."

The Luckiest Man in the World

At the premiere of his film, John said that if he had to make a choice between being physically whole or knowing God the way he does through his physical weakness, he would choose to remain as he is. ALS has brought him so very close to God that he would never want to give up this intimacy.

While John cannot take a physical step, he has already taken his first spiritual step into God's presence, where he lives on a daily basis because of his terrible disease. As you listen to John, you understand that when he calls himself "The Luckiest Man" in the world, he means this fifteen-year ALS wilderness journey with God has made him the most blessed man in the world. You see, the lucky wilderness is actually the blessed wilderness because it is through this that we enter into God's temple. John does not consider his wilderness a bad place; it's a blessed place—the very temple of God where he has gone every day for fifteen years to meet with Him and know Him as he never could any other way. Do not fear the wilderness, as John Paine once did. Fear missing the wilderness and not becoming "The Luckiest Man in the World."

CHAPTER 14

THE ULTIMATE WILDERNESS

"When they came to the place called the Skull, they crucified Him there..." (Luke 23:33)

AD 33, 9:00 A.M., Passover Friday, the Place of the Skull, a public place near Jerusalem. Many people were coming and going, some stopping to see what was happening, observing three men on crosses, two criminals with Jesus in the middle. A large crowd had followed the crucifixion detail out of the city to the place of execution, the place of the ultimate wilderness.

No one knew it was the ultimate wilderness on that spring morning. Not the Pharisees or the Sadducees, the instigators of the crucifixion. Not the high priests who brought the trumped-up charges against Jesus. Not Pilate, the Roman procurator who gave legal sanction to the sham crucifixion. Not the Roman soldiers, the innocent crucifiers who simply carried out their orders. Certainly not those who knew Jesus the best: the disciples, who were desperately afraid and completely confused. Not Mary, the mother of Jesus, whose pain and grief were beyond description. Not the beloved disciple John, who stood with Mary and sustained her through her ordeal. Clearly not Judas, the traitor, who, overwhelmed by the horror of what he did, went out and hanged himself. No one knew except for the One on the cross, Jesus, the Savior of mankind.

The Crossroads Crucifixion

The crucifixion was nothing like the romanticized and sanitized version we hear about. It did not occur on a green hill far away but on what appears to be a busy thoroughfare with people going about their business, hurrying to get things done before the Passover Sabbath when all commerce would stop for this high and holy day. It was a crossroads crucifixion, as all Roman executions were, deliberately carried out in public as a deterrent to disobedience to Rome. On that busy entrance into Jerusalem, a significant number of people stopped to see what was happening at Calvary, the "Place of the Skull."

Earlier, one such person, Simon of Cyrene, who was innocently coming into town from the country, had been pressed into carrying the cross beam to which Jesus would be nailed. Others read Pilate's words in Hebrew, proclaiming Jesus as the "King of the Jews," words he would not change. Passersby shook their heads in derision and hurled insults at Him. The robbers also heaped insults on Him until one of them repented and received the assurance of salvation that very day. The chief priests, elders, and teachers of the law mocked Him as He entered the ultimate wilderness.

What makes Calvary the ultimate wilderness? Of all the times in history when a man entered a dry and desolate moment in life, Calvary stands out as the worst. To be utterly innocent and yet die the death of the most guilty, to be totally powerful and yet die the death of the weakest of the weakest, to be the greatest of the great and yet die the death of the least of the least. What could be a more significant wilderness?

The agony of His wilderness began the night before in Gethsemane when He took His men with Him to His favorite escape in Jerusalem to pray. Here in the garden, He found strength to continue no matter what He faced. His men knew this was the place of peace for Him— that's how Judas knew where to find Him so the soldiers could arrest Him. His soul was devastated, sorrowful unto death itself. He needed support to make it, not only from His Father, but also from

His men. Yet they let Him down—they couldn't stay awake. It was a bitter taste of the wilderness to come. Clearly, He was disappointed in them. The one time He counted on them for strength and support, they forsook Him.

The Cry That Had to Be Uttered

On this sunny spring morning, the air was pierced with the screams of the suffering, the shouts of the crowd, and the taunts of the soldiers. Only Jesus had dignity, something that was true from the moment of His arrest right through the crucifixion. At noon on that day, darkness came over the whole land until three in the afternoon. The curtain between the Holy Place and the Holy of Holies in the temple, cutting off the entrance of man from the presence of God, was torn in two. A new way of intimacy opened between God and man through Jesus. The earth quaked, and graves opened, releasing their dead in resurrection. Around three o'clock that afternoon, Jesus entered into the depths of the ultimate wilderness when He cried out the most awful words in history: *"My God, my God, why have you forsaken me?"*

That's the ultimate wilderness: being forsaken by God. He knew the answer to His question. He knew why the Father had to turn away from Him, He knew He had become sin itself, and the holy God had to turn His back on His Son. The cry came from the deepest depths of His soul; He could not hold it back. The ultimate wilderness tore His very being even as that curtain was torn in the temple.

There is the human in this cry: *"My God, my God."* Jesus the man had been in unbroken fellowship with His Father all His life. God had been His God. He had lived in radical dependence on His Father through the Holy Spirit. He had done nothing apart from His Father, and His Father had continued with Him at all times. For the first time in His life, He could not find His Father; He was entirely on His own, and it was more than He could bear. The horrors of sin crushed His spirit in that awful moment.

Yet there was something even more overwhelming in that cry. It was not just the cry of a Man who lived a totally holy life and felt all the evil of sin placed on Him so His very identity became sin. It was the cry of the Man who *was* God. There's something infinite and eternal in that cry, something we can't begin to understand, but something we can try to describe. For all of eternity, He and the Father had been one in every way, one in ways we can never grasp. Now that infinite fellowship was broken by the infinite price the Father, Son, and Holy Spirit had to pay for our leadership. Yes, our leadership, our gifts and our opportunities came at the expense of the broken forsakenness Jesus suffered on the cross. It's as if the whole Trinity asked the same involuntary question, each knowing the answer— the Father asking, "Why must I forsake My Son?", and the Holy Spirit asking, "Why must We forsake the Son?" The Son forsaken, the fellowship of the Trinity broken. That's the price of the ultimate wilderness; that's the price of our sin, our life, and our leadership.

We cannot be small leaders centered on small goals, measuring ourselves in the small ways of our world. We must live up to the big price that the Father, Son, and Holy Spirit paid so we can be Their kind of leaders. We must pursue the zigzag line of life to fruitfulness. We can do this because Jesus entered the ultimate wilderness, death—and not just death, but death for sin, so we would never have to go there. The wilderness wanderings that we face lead to life, not death, because He entered our ultimate wilderness for us. He's the one who finally straightens out the zigzag life. All our leadership has to grow from this. It must be for Him, not for us. It must advance Him, not us. It must be for His purpose, not ours. It must be for His glory and no one else's. None of our wildernesses, no matter how painful, compare to His.

Zigzag to the Ultimate Destination

The zigzag line of life leads to the ultimate destination: resurrection. Yet resurrection is not just our ultimate destination; resurrection is our immediate destination, as well. Every time we enter a wilderness season when we seem to be wandering aimlessly in confusion, or we feel that life is over—our career has crashed or our ministry has ended—we find resurrection in the midst of our confusion. If we will trust God and His good purposes for us even when we can't see where we're going or understand what's happening to us, we can find strength to rise above our circumstances and anxieties and respond with a peace that no one understands. That's resurrection. We die many deaths on the zigzag line, but we can also rise from the dead as many times as we die. Unfortunately, far too many of us are like the Children of Israel who chose to die in the wilderness because they wanted to control their lives, refusing to trust God and take risk with Him. Christ has paid the price of death in our stead; we must pay the price of death in our pride. We must trust Him, rest in Him, and take risk with Him. That's how we get to His resurrection for us.

The fact that Jesus has faced the ultimate wilderness in our place and died in our stead must impact our lives and our leadership. We must be leaders in resurrection, leaders living out of our trust in the Father—not leaders dying under our own control. We must take the risk of resting in our Lord on the zigzag line of life, not wrestling in ourselves. When we take that risk—even when the worst happens and we fail or lose our leadership or our children suffer or we are publically humiliated—we have the certainty of resurrection in Christ. Jesus has passed through the ultimate wilderness for us.

The zigs and zags of the wilderness line leading to fruitfulness are resurrection way stations along the path to God's ultimate purpose for us: to usher us into His presence conformed to the image of

Christ. Our success is not His highest priority as it has been mine. He does not need our success to accomplish His aims; He can be successful entirely on His own. Conformity to Christ is what the zigzag line is all about; and while it often doesn't make sense to us, it does to our Father. He does not need our success, but He does want us to be successful in our accomplishments and in our character. That is why He has us on the zigzag line. There is a determinative connection between who we are and the fruit we bear. Unless we learn to trust Him, others will never trust us—and without the trust of our followers, there's only one thing we can do: fail.

As the curtain in the temple was torn, in order for us to enter freely into God's presence, so the curtain in our hearts must be torn for God to work freely in us. God has done everything He can to tear down that curtain, but it's up to us to take down the ragged and worn-out hindrance to God's power through us. We hide behind the tatters of a useless curtain and refuse to enter our ultimate wilderness with Christ. We refuse to face and deny self and take up the cross as Jesus called us to. Of course, we think we have taken up the cross, and undoubtedly we have many times. But until leadership is no longer about us, until the only stake we have in leadership is God's glory and the stain of self no longer scars our leadership, the tatters of that curtain remain in place.

Tear down that curtain. Jesus has entered the ultimate wilderness for us. Don't go there on your own. Go with Him beyond the ultimate wilderness to the ultimate fruit of the zigzag life: resurrection. Let the zigs and the zags of life bring you into His resurrection power so He can work through you. Then, at last, the zigzag life will become the shortest line to fruitfulness for you.

57910119R00043

Made in the USA
Columbia, SC
14 May 2019